Underwater Lengths in a Single Breath

Poems by

Benjamin S. Grossberg

The Ashland Poetry Press
Ashland University
Ashland, Ohio 44805

Grateful acknowledgment is made to those magazines in which these poems first appeared:

Alaska Quarterly Review: "West End of Dallas," "Amerigo Vespucci, 1506, Contemplates Another Sheet of Vellum"
Barrow Street: "Conclusion of a Poem Begun by Marlowe"
Green Mountains Review: "Drowning"
Nimrod: "Barely April," "One Last Thought" (as part of "Variations")
Malahat Review: "From the Water" (Leander) and "From the Shore" (Hero) as "This Hellespont," "Banana Flower," "Hudson Hallucinates a Final Letter Home"
Mid-American Review: "Antonio Remembers Sebastian"
Paris Review: "Icarus Considers" (as "Icarus Explains"), "Zharkov, Translated Sometime After the Year 2000," "Edgar at Supper, Fifty Years On"
Pleiades: "The Deer"
Poet Lore: "Last Conversation in Monticello, NY"
Seattle Review: "A Middle Class Consideration of Lust," "Secret"
Southern Poetry Review: "Between the Gods of Earth and Air"
Spoon River Poetry Review: "Renaissance Fair"
Tampa Review: "From the Shore" (Penelope)
Western Humanities Review: "The Fourteenth Piece," "A Brief Tour with Whitman," "The Man Who Had His Bone Marrow Irradiated Writes Jeanne Calment," "Compost," "Underwater"

"A Middle Class Consideration of Lust" and "A Brief Tour with Whitman" also appeared in the Alyson Publications Anthology *Gents, Bad Boys, and Barbarians.*

The author thanks the Cultural Arts Council of Houston and Harris County for a 1998 Emerging Artist Fellowship and the Ohio Arts Council for a 2003 Individual Artist Fellowship.

Thanks also to friends and teachers: Charles Derry, Ed Hirsch, Richard Howard, Dave Kajganich, Cynthia Macdonald, Karen

Nelson, Alan Michael Parker, Robert Phillips, Laurie Sheck, Paul Simmons, the Tuesday group, and Steven Young.

"Banana Flower" is for Rachel Castelino. "Icarus Considers" is for Sean Law.

Copyright © 2007 by Benjamin S. Grossberg

All rights reserved. Except for brief quotations in critical reviews, this book, or parts thereof, must not be reproduced in any form without permission of the publisher. For further information, contact the Ashland Poetry Press, Ashland University, Ashland, OH 44805.

Printed in the United States of America

ISBN: 978–0–912592–58–9

Library of Congress Catalog Card Number: 2006937892

Cover: A detail from "Hero and Leander" by William Etty

Photo credit, back cover: Dennie Eagleson

For Michael Bartha, Jason Bradshaw, and Cody Enloe

Contents

(Compost)/1

Icarus Considers/5
Hudson Hallucinates a Final Letter Home/7
Arrowhead/10
Underwater/12
Drowning/15
The Deer/18
A Middle Class Consideration of Lust/21
From the Water/23
From the Shore/25

Secret/29
Between the Gods of Earth and Air/31
West End of Dallas/34
Of Thoughts and Things/36
A Brief Tour with Whitman/38
Banana Flower/40
The Man Who Had His Bone Marrow Irradiated Writes
    Jeanne Calment/43
The Fourteenth Piece/45
Edgar at Supper, Fifty Years On/47

From the Shore/51
From the Water/53
Barely April/55
Last Conversation in Monticello, NY/59
Antonio Remembers Sebastian/61
Renaissance Fair/63
Zharkov, Discovered in 1997, Translated Sometime After the
    Year 2000/65
Amerigo Vespucci, 1506, Contemplates Another Sheet of
    Vellum/68
Conclusion of a Poem Begun by Marlowe/70

One Last Thought/75

We are past the time of myths, past a belief
in total regeneration; we have come to a time
when an ending can be unmediated, can be nothing
but an ending. Perhaps this is why I block
the Saturday, put off all the work that must get done,
and head around to the back of the shed.

It is grown over with brambles, alive and sharp,
curling around it like razor wire, but I can see
underneath: small chickenwire square, three foot
by three. And clearly there is something
under the brambles, variegated grays and browns,
but nothing, I think, rich as compost.
We are past the time of myths. Without
gardening gloves or shears, I uncoil the brambles.

It is Saturday. It is November. I have spent
the morning raking the season's leaves off the yard,
where they fell weeks ago. Now there are piles
each half as tall as a man and almost as disordered,
each somber and with a thousand holes
that somehow make an opaque surface.
This is what I need today: to define and divide
garbage from anything else, and to decide
what can be composted, what must be thrown away.

Beneath the brambles, I find sticks and rotted logs,
probably for an outdoor grill, a previous resident.
I do not know how many people rented this house
before me, but it occurs to me that I am peeling back
layers of past residents, from one who left brambles
to another who kept wood, which I define as garbage,
which does not belong in compost.
Though that, too, might break down eventually.

In the time of myths, everything could break down.
Everything could be taken in and absorbed, and something else
turned out, a pearl. We could take in a mouth full of poison
and spit out pure water, return to clean thought.

What is it that cannot break down on a compost pile,
what feelings have a half-life greater than our lives?
Combinations unnatural in the course of normal apprehension,
scattered like a handful of hot seeds on the compost, curl over
like bramble and razor wire. But I will try to remove
the razor wire, as I remove the wood, piece by piece,
and bundle it by the shed.

And there are leaves under that, and fire ants. The leaves
warp together like cardboard, gray, and the ants
are tiny red jewels. But I poke around,
brush the leaves to one side, and it is underneath
I find a ribbon of the other black gold, regeneration,
what the garbage has come to: years before I came
to this house, in the time of myths. I have no connection
to this inhabitant, and no clue but the rich blackness
of what he did here, and even that no clue, a void
as black as compost: only that he put in the right things
that managed to become nothing, or rather,
a nothing I could use.

We have no connection though we have lived
in the same house, and I will try, emptying armful
after armful of this season's leaves onto his compost,
and covering them thoroughly with his leavings,
to echo what he has done, in the time of myths:
to make no trace of my garbage, to commute
what is garbage into black gold,
to find for myself any workable myth.
I think, this is what animals do;
I think, this is what artists do;
I think, this is what God does.

Icarus Considers

There is no death in the sun. I know it will look far otherwise
to whoever watches from shore, to whoever stands

at the blue Aegean, pointing up at a mythical bird soaring too close
to the light, or those milling in markets who catch what must seem

to be a stone falling, or rather, a stone pitching a moment
as the last of my feathers fly away from me like tiny birds themselves,

each discovering individual flight, and the wax spills out,
hardens to lace as it falls back toward the ocean. I know

it will look like an image of failure. How could it not
with Daedalus leagues below me screaming himself hoarse,

jerking his earth-heavy body like a moth in an attempt to stabilize
his flight, shouting up that the sun will kill me? But there is no death

in the sun. At that height my lungs will fill with purer air
and I will meet the brightness like a lover. I will open my wings

and my eyes, which will, in a manner, burn with his face.
What else can it look like from a distance but failure,

how can anyone expect to understand from solid earth?
What falls away, what burns, is mere husk thrown off,

and I will emerge lighter, able to continue rising into his arms
without the trappings of wax and feathers, without the shouting

of Daedalus or the blue Aegean, where men
who don't understand will look skyward, shield their eyes

and see, or think they see, something impossible
in the clear sky—a domain they have surrendered to mythology,

birds, clouds and the beautiful, unreachable, life-giving sun—
light meeting light.

Hudson Hallucinates a Final Letter Home

1.
I watched the Half Moon recede. The men jeered me, threw
dirty chunks of ice, bits of rope, whatever they had.
They pointed and laughed, patted each other's backs, shouted
that I was free to find any passage I wanted now, that I wouldn't
need any help to run this ship. But before long I lost
their shouts, and the Half Moon, which filled the entire horizon
at twenty feet, faded

into the line of fog where the ocean meets the sky, as gray here
as dirty cotton, almost indistinguishable from the water.

At first it wasn't very cold or lonely. It seemed that they
were always about to come back, that any moment a speck
might distinguish itself in the horizon, tacking straight

for me, those same men, leaning over the edge, lowering
a rope, holding out grimed hands, smiling with their

blackened, broken teeth: *come back with us, come
with us now, back to England. Lift your hands to us now.*

2.
Hunger and night fell together. Though I don't remember
being cold for very long, or thirsty, before the metal gray sky
leached into my eyes. Even the skiff began to appear gray,
and my fingers and toes. I tried to recover the frost
off my eyelashes, and wondered if, in the cold, I would ever
see myself again, without these clothes, the map
of myself

with its own continental contours, its own northwest passage.
And if I did, would all of me be infected with gray, too.

After an hour or hours, or maybe days (the sun
never sets here, not for long, so it's hard to tell) I dipped
my hand in the water. Strangely, it wasn't cold

like you'd expect, but warm and thick, like seal oil.
I sat up and began to paddle with fury I didn't know I had.

There is a genius in the water, in the isolated gray world
of northwest ice, and he guided me. He took my hand.

3.
Whole worlds passed by. At first I moved slowly, watching
the gray of the water leach into my hand and travel up
my forearm and elbow, but then the spirit took the skiff
and we moved under three full sail. My hand and the ocean,
my hand and the water, guided by an unseen inspiration
and the infinite sensitivity of touch: I thanked them then,
my mutinous crew—

teaching me exploration, the waste of a boat and a hundred
men, floating on a coffin of wood. Just my body

and the endless ocean, that's all. Even the skiff hinders me,
and my clothes, and these excess layers of skin. Discovery
happens up close, with nothing disguising the undulations

of the water, without the distraction of food or any color
other than gray. The momentary stars were like miracles.

The water was warm as blood. And the air lingered out
my breath until a passage opened in the continent.

4.
White hills off in the horizon receded of their own, gathering
up their snows like skirts, revealing a warm water passage
underneath, where the dull gray brightens to silver in a rush
of movement. A crack in the continent, and Asia is there—
opening itself up like secret tapestried doors, like a silk fan

descending from delicate, painted lips. No skiff, no skin,
but swallowed by liquid—

the gray bled into my chest and lungs, washing even
my heart with the genuine element, until I could leak it

from my mouth, finger tips, the corners of my eyes,
all openings of me, falling like drops of ink. Do not expect
to see me again, to kiss me in Bristol, or kneel while I

am received by James. I am my element. Don't mourn
this perfect frozen composure on the ice. I am here,

Katherine, still here, tracing a solitary path above
continents, finding a sea large enough to carry my name.

Arrowhead

So much of the day was spent just walking
around the site: from the art tent to the pool,
from the pool up the hill, to the small theater
or the woods that separated camp
from Tenant, and, not two miles away,
the mental hospital, biggest in the state.
I was fourteen and immature for my age.
It was beautiful there.

Toward the end of first summer session
I met him. He must have been fourteen, too,
give or take a year, thin and taller than I was,
with braces, black curly hair and the beginnings
of a bad complexion. It was almost magic
how we became friends, maybe three days
before we buddied up at everything: dynamite,
war, or splashing in the pool.
What a relief it is to find a friend, how strange
the extent to which the notion of incompleteness
is itself incomplete until coupling comes
and you realize (how different camp seemed)
what you were missing.
I can't remember his name.

The third to last day, we sat on a picnic table
straight from swimming, bathing suits dripping,
towels around our necks, and two girls
were making fun, I think teasing us about
something that led him to pretend—
to hang his towel on his arm like a cloak
and hold it between us and them, and pretend—
to kiss me, but barely pretend, our lips
brushing so close I could feel the fuzz
against my face, could almost feel
his delicate black lashes closing.

What were the girls saying? I know only
that it hadn't upset me before; we were
laughing, sitting on the table laughing
(maybe with them) but then the towel
fell and sunlight broke between us.

When I remember this incident
part of me sees . . . maybe Kevin, as he was,
but another part imagines him older:
thirty-five, clear skin, dark eyes and curly hair,
holding the towel to make a small pool of shade.
And though there are just a few inches
in the space between the towel and his face,
it seems like a whole world distilled,
a world he creates for us, between
the trees, the laughter and the sun,
all of what bears down from the outside.
Though we don't quite kiss, in my second memory
we don't have to, and it's better
that we don't. The moment continues
until we forget the silence, and I reach out
to the nightstand, and he pulls up the covers,
and neither of us has to say good night.

Underwater

The struggle comes only at the start. Though the first lap
is easy, the second abruptly turns hard. The ache
in my legs advances down my ankles, my arms take the burden
of all forward movement, and when I breathe
I see how low I sink in the water. Four slow laps like this
and stopping is all I think about. Nothing's
natural here. Humans don't have webbed feet or gills.
We don't have sleek bodies or coats that repel water well.
Even tamed and indoors, regulated, heated, guarded
and chlorinated, this element retains a little will of its own.
Or maybe it's just that gravity starts to seem like volition.
(In any case, the pool begins to taste like a petty ocean.)

How about love at first sight? Love really happens
at second sight, or third. The first movements are all about
newness, the barely conscious decision to relinquish
yourself to what's unseeable, impossible to hold.

The middle laps are easy. They are what can't be
remembered. And that is due to the rhythm of breathing
and the clockwork sound of the right hand plunging in
followed by the quieter sweep of the left.
Plunge, sweep, breathe, repeat: focus and movement.
Consciousness may remain, but it is absorbed, forced
from stroke to stroke, wholly lost in repetitive action.
The element is solid now, tucking lower
under the body, bearing it up, like a parent holding
a child by the stomach as he learns to swim. It is gentle
on the chest and thighs. Weightlessness is more
than a physical sensation; the pool moves the body.

How about reading and the awful slowness
of the first few pages of anything? When does the story
stretch its print fist off the page, grabbing the reader
by the shirt collar, shaking off the action of turning pages?

The final laps are memorable again, though hard
in a different way. The limbs don't complain
as they did during the first laps. They dutifully recite
the lines you are not feeding them, obey orders
immediate and ungiven. But there is fatigue, a hollowness
which will stiffen later. There is pain without hesitation
so that finally the intellect must intervene to remind
the body what pain means. Laps take shape again.
There is no sense of accumulation, but distance
has been traveled; it is embodied in some number. The world
resolves into better focus now, a child sliding on his first
pair of glasses. Like me at thirteen, sliding on mine—

Where the body has been is unclear, but now it is in a pool.
A radio is playing and people are sitting on the side, talking.

Two old men are wading through the lane on the right.
Swimming lessons (loud, echoing laughter) occupy

the lane to the far left. A swimmer to the immediate left
is doing the breast stroke. And underneath me—

this could have been going on for half an hour—
a fortyish man in a sheer blue Speedo swims underwater

lengths in a single breath, elegant lines against the pale
pool floor. His arms expand up and his legs open,

then both sweep closed in an underwater current,
the way an underwater current might sway coral

or jar a school of fish. He is beautiful: thinning
black hair, broad back creasing and uncreasing

with minutely defined musculature. His face
must be as warm as the water feels, with eyes

*the same liquid blue. A siren waits to descend
lower and lower as I swim down to him,*

*well past the pool's concrete bottom, until I lose
track of the last gasp of oxygen bubbling up*

*from my lips. Even well out of arm's reach,
even from up here, he is beautiful: the hook*

*in the text; love discovered. He is
the glimpse which justifies the risk.*

Drowning

1.
Choose your element. The thin tissues of the lungs
can drink it in, soak it up like shredded rag.
Choose your medium: be a drowning artist.
Drown in tempera, drown in porcelain, drown in the roles
or instruments that you play. Do not begin slowly;
that is not the way with drowning. Thought will
freeze you into inaction. Close your eyes, open
your mouth, unconstrict the tube of your throat.
Breathe it in. Drown as a means of coping with life,
or not coping. Drown in time: let days overwhelm you.
Find no compromise between maddening, ruinous action
and inactivity on which you bob and float lifeless.
Breathe it in. Drown in desire. Find those objects
which promise only sustained wanting, and swim
into the sea of them; grab the element hand over hand
barely managing to stay afloat, and still nothing,
beautiful nothing, remains with you. Breathe it in.
Drown in what you have lost. This is easiest.
Let the loss crest around your face, taste its saltiness,
travel down to feel the silt bottom with your palm.
It is a Marianna Trench; you have been dead for hours
yet you are still drowning, still traveling down
in darkness toward those creatures who have evolved
without help from the sun. Breathe it in.
Take the image with you into death. Discover heaven
a clear liquid that saturates your lungs with air,
in which the desire for immersion may be
sustainably met. Breathe it in; cough it up.
You can drown in sex and love, but those
are child's games. They only distract you
from the elements which flow beneath them
like denser water. You can also drown in yourself.
(This has the advantage of not requiring other people.)

2.
Amniotic fluid is another ocean: landlocked, dark, domed
by living skin as far away as night sky. Suspended
in so much liquid what is there to do but drown?
What does a baby know when the aperture cracks
and a splash far off—its hearing still sonar like the ears
of a whale—indicates that the bathwater is draining,
the ocean is draining: an invasion of light and air.
What does a baby's body know of how to react?
There is knowledge implicit in the flesh. I was there,
in the interface of air and water, and cast my lot
securely with the depth and the darkness, opened
my mouth to drink in what remained of the draining
fluid. The impetus to drowning kept the baby
in the hospital four months, a body too small
to live outside a body, lungs drying, warping
like cardboard, hands permanently wrinkled and aged
by the element, and everything too sensitive, too new,
imperfect, crying out for darkness and warmth, salt
and ambergris, even the new skin somehow unready.
This is more than temptation; this has the contours
of a life. Drown in the heat of a summer evening;
drown in the tears of sweat pooling down your neck
onto your shoulders as you think of desires that will
never be met. Cast lots only once, and early,
and spend an entire life sifting through the outcome;
breathe it in. A baby trapped under glass watches
a figure hover against a background of artificial light—
she is too dry, too bright to be its mother—
baby who has made a choice sudden and early
and wonders how it is possible that a sea
can spit you out, like Jonah in the inner ocean
of whale blood, spit out onto hard gravel,
baby who will live many lifetimes, each ended
by drowning, each renewed by impact with the shore.
Death, love, loneliness, fear or time. Don't
be fooled by the element; the element doesn't matter.
Baby who will remember nothing of the plastic

and the glass, of the tubes, who will grow from half
amphibian to full man, who will retain only
a thirst for immersion, a temptation to drowning,
nothing of the incident but the impulse.

The Deer

You have to be running in winter, in the snow, when the snow
is falling, and better if it is toward dusk, when light
seems to drain into the snowfall, making it brighter.

You must be in the woods, trees arcing above you, following
an untrimmed path, the packed snow absorbing your footfall
as fully as the falling snow absorbs light. Now

snow is the element: you are just another suspended thing,
moving thing that seems suspended. You too are absorbing
light as the sun sinks beneath the gray felt of the sky,

absorbing wind high in the trees, the branches entwining
like fingers. You must run long enough to forget
the pain in your knee, which you have wrapped

tightly, your hands which sting beneath your gloves, your
face stiff with the frozen breath puffing up from your lips.
You must in fact get to that place in running

where you forget everything except the element: where you
fall forward as effortlessly as the snow, sway like
the trees, which sway as if they responded to music

they themselves generated, each individually
and together. You must hear only this particular music.
Here is what happened:

> *A family of deer. There were four along the path,*
> *tripping about each other in finely-haired*
> *auburn grace. Their legs ran high up their bodies*
> *which were arced and brown, each with*
> *the elongated balance of a dancer. They circled,*
> *kicked their back legs high above them,*
> *returned like a chorus in the vast movement*
> *of the woods. And when I came on them,*

> *my pace and breathing even, they let me pass*
> *just a yard, two yards to their left—*
> *playing until I came within twenty feet,*
> *then becoming still in the falling snow,*
> *the only still thing for a mile around,*
> *near enough to brush with my fingers.*

But that didn't happen at all.

> *I saw them from a hundred feet, barely able to focus*
> *without my glasses, before I realized, yes, at eighty feet:*
> *there were four. But instead of starting at my footfall,*
> *loosing themselves from the clearing, arrows*
> *shot at different angles into the woods,*
> *they simply pulled back, retreated behind*
> *the snowfall farther and farther down the path.*
> *Alive to the moment of snow, they were brown*
> *in a way that made brown hot and bright, until*
> *brown itself, how it can be cut with fine white spots,*
> *became a kind of inspiration. Their limbs seemed*
> *fantastically high and flexible, made to taunt*
> *a runner with the illusion of continuous movement.*
> *At seventy feet I saw that I was still at eighty feet,*
> *that they were moving laterally and higher*
> *in their jumps, but pulling to a constant distance—*
> *this continued for three miles before they scattered.*

But it didn't. That didn't happen either.

> *They never scattered. They watched*
> *with polished coal, their eyes a black liquid*
> *that wouldn't freeze. They led me along,*
> *seduced me forward for miles, until my joints*
> *rusted over and I fell on the snow, knees*
> *shattering the frozen earth like a dead weight.*
> *Unable to run farther, I looked forward, saw them*
> *linger there, kick in place. Their muscles, even*
> *the largest one's, so taut and young, dazzled*

> *with the possibilities of motion. They waited*
> *for me to get up as they bounded about each other,*
> *for me to rejoin the swaying trees, the lace*
> *of upper branches, the element of snow.*
> *They watched snow accumulate on my shoulders,*
> *watched cold move into my body, watched*
> *as my body drank the blue fluid into its core,*
> *my lips blue, skin blue, blue eyes frozen open.*

I don't know what happened. I saw them, then the miles
passed too quickly, flashed by so quickly that only my watch
assured me that I had run at all, that over an hour had passed—

and my fingers, which couldn't curl around the car key,
and my legs; I could barely walk. Also there was a vision
of deer: four of them, their nimble kick, their back legs

extending their whole bodies, making them flex like a single
lean muscle, instructing me with a laughterless ecstasy—
this is the way a body can run. I don't think I made them up,

but I was there, back at the car, silence dispersing over
its churning engine, and hadn't seen them go. Where were they?
Where are they now? Where in the snow had they gone?

A Middle Class Consideration of Lust

Olden days? I picture in cream and black
like a '20's movie, two men with round glasses
in summery bow-tied suits, sitting
across from each other in a train compartment
steaming through Great Plains states,
each with his nose in a small book:
Shelley, Byron, *Dr. Ansell's Headache Cures*—
who knows? Furtive, peering out like mice,
shielded by directions and dosages of quick
silver—eye contact happens: slicked hair
becomes tousled, and perhaps the scene
fades on one hand running around a shoulder,
flipping off the other man's jacket—
but real life doesn't fade: sure as sugar both
trousers come down.

It's different now, of course. At a gas station
in Memphis, my brother filled his van tank by hand
pump. His hippie hair and unwashed face, fumes,
the wet heat of the south, there must have been
romance somewhere. A man walked by him
from off the street, right by—within four feet
passed before him, close enough to smell
my brother's hair, oily enough to punch through
the petrol. At the perigee of the two bodies,
the soft word "blowjob" filled the vacuum
between them. I have to admire the guy's courage,
but somehow the train seems nicer
(would, even if it involved my brother).

And then there are extremes: horrified first-
year college student, I read that the library
bathrooms would be shut down because of—
of—"glory holes"—
which, bored through the metal stall walls
by pure determination (I guess), served

for romantic access—like rodent-size gates
to heaven. The front-page story
included a picture beneath the caption—
"Alexander Bathrooms Closed"—of one such wall,
writing too grainy to read, holes clearly visible.
Someone must have kept it, taped it in a diary
to remember, blushing—coy and fond, and why
not? It really is just a question of degree;

my last encounter was no less
sleazy. Sure, we'd exchanged rings, but I
didn't want him anymore, couldn't
remember if I ever had. Fully conscious of this,
I kissed the back of his neck and undid
his trousers with my right hand (fumbling my own
with the left). We were forty minutes
rhythmic as a washing machine, scant, oily,
and nearly without kisses. In the bathroom after,
he said, "I feel used."
I leaned down and kissed his face,
insides coiled like an over-wound watch,
not wanting to prolong contact.
I said, "I love you, sweetheart," barely
brushing his shoulder, "and I wish you wouldn't
feel that way." About an hour later he
kissed me goodbye, and we haven't spoken since.

From the Water

How awful it must have been: after twenty years
at sea, after movement and surprise—
what could a wife offer to compare
to the singing of strangers, women seen
only myopically, posing against each other
on a bare rock jutting up from the ocean?
Does their hair hang over their shoulders?
Who knows: you squint, you see
what you desire, you sail past, listening
and squinting. Manatees or sirens,
they are sirens, they are sirens.

You lose men. Of course you lose men.
You lose men who turn out to be pigs
waiting merely for the revelation, the release
of Circe's wand; you lose men to the teeth
of a cyclops: men who were from the beginning
fashioned for some creature to cut
his teeth on; you lose men overboard; you
somehow do not lose your ship.
And therefore the losses become
a kind of delight; you take pride in them.
You marvel how the ship moves forward.

You miss home. Who wouldn't?
Home becomes an ideal: a wife who moves
her fingers so deftly over the strings
she ought to be playing the lyre. But the strings
are bright, are colors, and she is weaving—
as she always was, even before you left—
your burial cloth. She is beautiful. Her body
is fixed in your mind like a navigation star:
you go northwest by her shoulders; you go east
to the taper of her fingers; you tack at her lips,
coast at her heels: her body,
a nation of nights in which you

do not sleep alone, in which her body,
always your lodestar, becomes your port.

And yes, it is lonely on deck. It is lonely
with a crew who are part of your journey
peripherally, so many, in a way nearly
indistinguishable. But you taste the Cattle
of the Sun; you make love to Calypso;
you leave Calypso; you have both the ideal
and the resurgent pleasure of newness—
it is lonely, sure. But you discover
relatively quickly that loneliness is salt,
in the right quantity enhancing everything
and part of what it means to live with the sea.

So there it is, and how awful: Ithaka—
do not be thankful. Kill the suitors; it is
what you came to do. Then love your wife.
Love her until you have exorcised
every last image of her beauty
from your head. And stay—
for even weeks. But then, old as you may be,
wise if that's what you want to call it, remember
Calypso, remember women on a bare island
of the Dodecanese, remember Polyphemus
even as an abandoned old friend—
and go off, go off again, to be at home—
as you've always been—when looking for it.

From the Shore

Today
        the cloth is a scene from early on, when I,
when he was young. We slept outside though it was cold,
to be near the trees, the rough face
                              of a rocky cliff,
and woke nearly covered in frost, frost on our eyelids,
snow on our hair, warm only
                              in those places our bodies
touched. Here I weave us waking: moving
                                      in to each other
as we did in sleep, but now moving in and away,
pushing our hands above our heads as if to push away
the sky, bending, warming
                              in movement. The sun
is just up. This image I will weave for days. I will
meditate on it; I will
                      choose threads for their
emotional color; I will work until my fingers seem
to move of their own volition, plunking and fretting
the strings with their own music. And then—
                                              I wake
in this—
        a kind of mania takes over. I find one thread
that isn't right, or fifty, and at first I gently undo
the texture, but my hands
                          turn greedy, turn ravenous,
pick at the yarn like carrion birds. They squawk
and attack, pull back and return, and I find
again
        an empty loom, and beside me, the carcass
of an image, memory
                        reduced to its component
vectors, to slips of color
                            that take meaning altogether
or not at all. I clean up the pieces; I go to sleep;
I wake the next morning with another image.

Tomorrow
                  it will be from later on: the picture
oppresses me already. It is late; he is
                                  leaving
to burn some cities, fight a battle, get away from me
however he decides to describe it. And I
will recall
              our last confrontation, at a meal, looking
up into his face, his red beard, eyes
                                  full of love,
knowing that he is lying. Marriage, too,
is an island kingdom, but once you leave you
                                      cannot
come back. I will take the image with me. They
will ask how I am progressing, and I will sit fixed
in a trance of making. They ask
                        if it's done, admire
my breasts and his cattle, my legs
                            and his land, but
it is the nature of obsession never to be done. They ask
why it takes so long, half a scene
                        in the woods, half
a beautiful face lying. I am making myself
sleepless, an old woman
                        who weaves with arthritic hands,
whose fingers are knotted like string. And that, of course,
takes decades. I wish I could marry one of them, marry
any of them—   finish with a memory, just one,
fold it into the pattern of the cloth, and then fold
the cloth itself, bury it, bury
                          him, and move on.

Secret

Things tumble out of control. A butterfly
in the South Pacific flutters its yellow wings
and days later a cold front forms over Tripoli,
moving north into the Balkans. Three weeks
later it's raining in Houston. Maybe I

had planned to walk to the park that day;
maybe you had hoped to get your car washed.
The process accelerates. A California
spear crab was brought to Florida in 1972,
a pet in a child's beach pail. "It can't stay,"

his mother said when he showed it to her
on the tile floor. She could have crushed it
beneath a single heel. "Take it to the shore;
let it go." By 1987, government estimates
were in the millions. Does this matter

to the woman in Baton Rouge who learns
a way to serve them blackened and, through
clever marketing and charm, soon earns
enough to send her youngest to college?
To the middle-aged kitchen hand who burns

his forearm on a blackening skillet?
He doesn't have insurance. That same day,
you and I find ourselves in a restaurant
having a tense talk over spear crab and red
wine. You've never tasted anything like it.

Were you the child holding the beach pail?
Maybe I was. Maybe the kitchen hand
burned himself preparing our meal.
Was it the rainstorm that prompted us to go
out at all? The same weather pattern will

circle the globe; next month it may batter
Houston like a tidal wave. Here's the point:
I know something I shouldn't. It doesn't matter
how. It's about one of your closest friends.
He's infected. The rest is just clutter.

Between the Gods of Earth and Air

Charon the ferryman leans
                    against a wharf railing
in light rain; it's just after midnight, warm,
and the black waves are knocking
                    the pylons, setting
his vision in a gentle back-and-forth motion.

                              It's all water.
Everything.
          The river, the misty sky, and most of all
memory. Was there a time he had skin,
                         a surface
capable of feeling? He runs his knuckles
along his collar bone just to hear
                         the calcium scrape.

Persephone sits on a shoal
                    just over the river.
She's part of the tragedy, curling
                    a finger in her hair,
wondering
          why Hades has become so dispassionate,
letting her toes make small circles in the water.

Perhaps she never loved him.
                    But there had been
pageantry at first—the feel of his dark heat against her
chest and thighs,
          and extended walks arm in arm,
surveying his gray domain.

                    And what is it like above?
The vicissitudes of a sad pantheon. Artemis hunts
the gray wolf in the Americas,
                    refusing to return

to the fold for all Zeus's calls,
                              and Mars has taken
to reading Dostoevsky in the bathroom, bored

with simple binaries
                    and the logic of rape.
Zeus himself has surrendered thunder and listens
to the patter of rain
                    from atop the clouds, dangling
his bare feet in the open air.

                              No tone of panic,
no dancing in the woods. Above or below. And
here, between the rocks
                        and clouds? What is here?
The gods have evolved with us into
the latest century, one by one falling
                                       to watching

themselves or the human
                        world around them, distant
and impersonal, like television. They pattern
themselves:
           aunts who don't write, children denying
prodigality its glamour, fathers and mothers

lighting incense in the living
                              room, stoking
the remote control like a laurel wand, stuck
in the cool, easy trance of worship.

                        And here,
between the gods of Earth and Air?

                              Charon feels
rain falling in his eye sockets, filling and rolling
down
     on the inside—a steady drip
from his shoulders, fingertips and ribs.

                        Persephone
kneels by the bank to see her face in the moving

river. With the distortion, it is like a moon—
though of course there is no moon
                                radiant with
reflected light, only her face. She thinks
                                        if she stares
at it long enough, she may become a rose.

West End of Dallas

Eighteen months ago a stranger went home with a hustler and
now he and I are leaning on a railing in the West End district
of Dallas in front of a restaurant neither of us can afford

and he's telling me about the hustler because he's absolutely
sure that this was the moment, that it only takes one exposure
and besides, he was careful every other time.

We have just met and he's unraveling himself for me
and I find myself asking "What's wrong with your hands?"
because they are scarred, maybe from terrible acne,

and he's telling me he told the hustler to wear a condom, saw
the hustler put it on—saw him—and the next day found it
stuffed between cushions in the front-room sofa, unused.

The West End is like a street fair. There are Hare Krishnas
here and they are slapping tambourines and chanting,
doing a dance which jerks them into each other,

and as he's talking tourist couples are moving
toward us, toward the railing. It is like driving
in a snowstorm. Only he remains stationary and tells me:

"I was careful every other time and I never had a hustler before.
It was a really weak moment and I knew him, you know.
He was a friend. He even said he didn't want to

go home with me because he respected me too much."
His eyes trace the red brick of the restaurant's walls
and I look at the people passing

out pamphlets—for Christian revival. It will happen later,
twenty minutes later, that he and I will be
talking to a red-haired girl of seventeen with blue,

cornflower blue, clear Texas afternoon
sky blue eyes—I don't know but they were like glass—
about God and she will say with a smile as beautiful

as the first man I tried to make stay with me,
"Hell exists. It is real." Neither of us will agree—
nodding our heads above her, bright as a Christmas angel.

When she sees there is nothing left to be said, she will ask
to pray with us. And he will say "no—"
suddenly angry, suddenly furious. We will walk away

from her, side by side in a cold trance. I won't know
what he is thinking but part of me will wish
we had stayed a minute longer and held her hand

if that's what she wanted. It is because I am
scared to hold his, scared of what the scars might be
and how they would feel on my palm.

Of Thoughts and Things

Mint or sea foam? I'd hedge, say "pastel green"
and point to where the label on the back guarantees
"hand woven."
Spotless, too, or if the fibers are a little rough
with wear, you'd have to get down on all fours
to notice, inspect it
with the beady eyes of an estate-sale shopper:
appraising stains, the lining, tracing each flower
that laces the border
for any flaw that might lower the price. I found
none. The chandelier was also beautiful,
and the crystal—
I say, "whoever lived here had wonderful taste."
A man, drooping mustache, stick thin,
salt-and-pepper
hair, sits at the cash box: "Yes; he's dead."
I figured he was dead. The quality of taste was
a dead giveaway,
and my neighborhood, and the antique bedroom set—
all of it suggested a delicacy beyond ready cash,
someone who studied,
collected and loved. I ask, "Did you live here?"
"No, no, the guy who lived here is dead."
I nod my head
as if he'd cleared up a misunderstanding, and pick up
one of the filigreed spoons. Here, he must have seen
the concave reflection
of his face a hundred times without pausing to notice,
and here, in a butter knife, a slash of his smile.
The silver shows
me now, eyebrows knitted, wondering what
I'd have to sacrifice to use these at my next holiday.
I'm above the mantle
too, standing by the maroon tapestry wing back
in which a man doesn't sit, legs crossed beneath
his hospital gown,

holding a crystal goblet filled with red wine,
listening to something on his tape deck, still unsold.
At his feet
lies a rug, maybe this one—pastel green, beautiful
and now perfectly natural beneath my black desk.

"Did you know him?" I ask, taking three twenties
from my wallet and handing them across the table.
The guy says no
and shrugs his shoulders. Sometimes we speak
of walking in someone's footsteps; every day, ten
times, fifty times,
literally, I'll walk in his, across one of the pieces
of his life that has been released back into the general
flood, what defined
him in aggregate, but betrays nothing of him now,
so much a part of this room, you couldn't tell
his taste from mine.
I've furnished it with second-hand things, garage-sale
desk, five-dollar chair, an old brass lamp without a shade—
and more than that,
much more, so much it would take pages to list.
And now this rug underlies it all, shifted from one collector
to another
with a little cash. So what if the house, if every room
is full of ghosts, and you have only to squint to see them
walking back and forth
through the small confines, running gossamer fingers
over picture frames? Fifty dollars for the rug,
and it is beautiful,
and I walk happily in his footsteps; he joins me
for breakfast, reclines in one of my chairs, his thin arms
breaking through
the gown sleeves to raise his crystal goblet
to me now, and my turn, and my world of thoughts,
and my world of things.

A Brief Tour with Whitman
NYC, 1994

Pull up your pants, Walt! God, give the boy
a tenner and—sorry, I thought you—
There you are, come along, there's more to see—
Mill around, eye contact won't commit you.
If anyone touches you in a way you don't like,
let them know; don't be shy—
no, that's not your problem—
The booths are against the wall; you have to pay, yes,
I know, but it's only a few dollars. You should have
shaved your beard; most of us like a smooth face.
Don't bristle, just avoid spikes if you don't want to
get hurt. This is what you wanted to see, Walt—
the bloom of an indicative bud, or perhaps past the bloom,
maybe the fruit, overripe, of an indicative flower—
It's the love of comrades.

Come on! Don't linger, Walt! Everything
changes, I know. The glassy surface of wet asphalt,
smoke from the sewers, the smell—damp garbage?
maybe stale pretzels?—you'll like this place better—
we can sit on a bench and listen to traffic.
See the statue of manly love? I always think the neck
on the one sitting looks too thin. Like gauze, aren't they?
And that—womanly love! You can see the breasts
beneath her shirt. Do you see the glances here, too—
the embraces, lingering touches of one for the one
he loves, as they must part? Let me hold your hand, Walt.
Cold? It's the rain. You know, I could kiss you here
and it would be all right. I could even hold your
woolly head in my lap and that would be all right, too.
But come! Right across the street! There's more—

This is The Monster, Walt, actually the second one.
The first was built out on Fire Island, near your own
Paumanok; it was so successful they opened this other—

Dancing's downstairs. It's all right; he's the bouncer.
I'll need ID. Your beard will do—
Comrades! They are all comrades. Most, happy to be.
Away from the bar, yes, follow me, yes—
indeed, these *are* the roughs, these *are*—the piano,
sleek, black, here for us, and the men gathering round.
Sit, though of course you won't know the songs.
I'll be right back—
Here. Good, put your elbows up, let your beard fall
on the lid, lean in—To the City of Comrades!
Now drink, but not too slow.
There are other places for us to visit—

Not like soldiers, are they? Thinner, more like gauze
than the plaster casts, and be careful where you touch, Walt.
Don't touch any broken skin, avoid touching
any sort of fluid or—wait, put these on.
They're a little powdery inside, they'll make
your hands sweat—but you won't notice after a while.
These are the wounded comrades—
one tube runs under his gown; the other pumps
into his arm. God no, he's thirty-eight.
Kneel, talk to him a little. If you want
you could spend the night. Just don't touch him
with exposed skin, be careful of the needles,
if he wakes, don't tax him with too much excited blather—
he'll tire easily—maybe just stay.
I'll dim the light and come for you in the morning.

But before I go, listen—
I know it's all stressed and strained, running,
and calamus roots have become arteries
to our hearts—whether we know it or not—but
it's the nature of purity, of reality, and besides
there really is more to see. Don't give up
now, Walt—there's more to see, much
more to see—
and I'm sure it would be better if you stayed.

Banana Flower
after Lawrence

You would like to throw a banana at me?
Go ahead, they are conveniently boomerang shaped.

Actually, you may not. These are not ripe.

To one born here, perhaps this is common—
a banana tree. Or banana bush. But I
have never seen one before, and never seen this:
so big and red, I grin when I touch the tip.

Big, red, thick and heavy—
not open, not there for any slovenly comer
to look inside, but all out, ponderous and pendulous,
a big red flower dangling from the bush,
bigger than my two fists, solid as a sinker,
suitable only to rest in my palm.

There, I am grinning again.

This is not fit for a vase.

This is not, indeed, a flower for women
as the movies portray them, not likely
to lodge behind the ear or lie supple
as a wrist corsage. This is absolutely
a man's flower, to be carried in the fists of men
with no accommodation to any sort of uniform:
cowboy hats, big buckles and ironed denim of the south,
leather jackets, chaps and snap-on rings of the north,
boots of any type.

Maybe it would be a good thing, too,
getting men to carry and exchange flowers,
palming and clutching banana flowers, everywhere
flowers in men's hands. Everywhere. Supermarkets.

Maybe it would take some weight off
more wanton forms of affection.

Not that I have anything against sex.

But I have courted some danger, made quite a few
mistakes that I probably wouldn't have made
had I been clutching a banana flower.
Carrying and exchanging the flowers,
big and red, heavy, masculine. In supermarkets. Libraries.

And there's a smell that radiates from them, fog and musk.
Humidity makes it hard to tell where the smell ends.

On the ground are petals, red, tear-shaped peels,
tough as canvas, maybe half a dozen.
I see now how the flower shrinks
as the bananas ripen. As the bananas grow
longer and the bunch extends down, the flower unpeels,
unpetals, layer by layer. Until there is nothing left.

And what do we do when that happens?

If men are exchanging them, using them
as romantic symbols, pinning them to their lapels
with big pins?
What to do, when we've decided to give each other
banana flowers and they fall apart?

It's okay with the flowers;
when they're gone, there are bananas to eat.
Dozens of bananas.
So there is always something left
with flowers.

But what do we do when our petals
are gone and the rest of the men,
intent on clutching and exchanging flowers
with younger men, ignore us?

What do we do when we disinherit
the very thing all of us become?

Even quite young banana flowers
have fewer petals than new ones.

What can we do when there's always someone with more?
And every day we are losing the few we may have left?
And still, we disinherit the very thing we'll all become?

—Houston

The Man Who Had His Bone Marrow Irradiated Writes Jeanne Calment

Jeanne Calment, now the world's oldest person at 120. . . .
—Reuters, 12/29/95

1.
I woke relieved of the weight of my bones, sprang from the hospital bed in an impossible arc, ripping the tubes out of my arm and from underneath my gown, sending the sheets flaring up about me like an accompaniment of angels. And after the superhuman effort to open my window, I stood looking down from the eighteenth floor.
                    This is San Francisco. The wind funnels in and around me. Shall I step out? Be taken by the air until I can locate the Gulf Stream, direct myself by opening the wings of my gown? Indistinguishable from the clouds, myself billowing, I want to glide over the Texas desert and feel slaked over the Caribbean, and over the Atlantic, feel warm salt air rise beneath my stomach, suspended between the ocean's blue like black, and the black which looks like blue.
                            I will be in Arles for spring, Jeanne. To visit you. Wear your best dress and wait for me with roses.

2.
We will stroll around town hand in hand, circling the new daffodils which we will barely see for our memories. I'll tell you about Freehold, how they clustered around my grandmother's mailbox yellower than they've been since, and you'll describe the bunch a doughboy thrust at you before a hurried kiss and train ride to the Marne.
                            But even if we can't see the daffodils, we will see each other: for me, white hair so sparse your powdery scalp shows through and what one hundred and twenty-one springs does to human skin, and for you . . . how thin I have become, how my ribs are visible almost to my underarms. And though nearly ninety years separates us—and an ocean, a culture and a language—mostly we will see our reflections at Arles.
                        Beyond the unstable quantities of stature, feature, and gender, we're the same, Jeanne. You and I are ageless.

3.
We will sit across from each other in your parlor, drinking weak tea
and chatting over lace, telling each other secrets about time that only
you and I can know. The possibility of death, the impossibility of life—
we will cover the great subjects nibbling lemon squares, clutching
on tattered shawls, forgetting
                                    to take our pills, our proper suppers,
becoming nothing but our talk, barely noticing when the sun
stops brightening the lowered shade on the parlor window, when
the room settles from gray to black and our voices retreat to a whisper,
gently forgetting as we settle into sleep, or something like sleep,
that may or may not be broken by the distant voices of the grandfather
clock, the hungry cat, the phone—
                                      but who would call? And still
undisturbed in our soundless, constant talk, when the sun comes up.

4.
I will not visit you in Arles for spring. There is still too much left
of my bones, and I have been grafted to hospital machines.
I remain part of this interchange of fluids, barely part of the vague
possibilities of sitting up, standing, walking, laughing, running,
and beyond all of these, a cure.
                                  Stay in your rocker with tiny joyful
eyes. Have the nurse bring you a metropolitan paper, and read about
me, just as I have read about you, twice over the wire service—
a birthday and a land deal. Read the strange science about platelets
and white cells, baboons and the thinness of my blood, and picture
me in bed, sometimes with the blinds open, sometimes preferring
total dark, but constantly caught
                                    in this blinding-white hospital
room, in the hard tension between finishing up and beginning.

The Fourteenth Piece

I found compassion by the river. That was his heart—also completely
physical, violet and red, trailing arteries. And I found his pain

in an adder's nest, his sleek, black liver underneath the eggs. It felt
like wet fish in my fist. I found and felt all of him

in intimate connection: his care, in the form of his large, stiff hands
set before an old woman, framing her weaving; and his love for me,

his lips and the lower half of his jaw—in its own way, once capable
of killing thousands—still warm and soft, disconnected, still life

if not alive itself. All of him, I found and felt all of him.
Except the fourteenth piece, which Typhon tossed in the river

Nile, hazel and soft, unaccustomed in his palm like fish in open air,
their round bellies and tails—his lenses, the tiny spheres,

and all the fine red filaments hanging off. In the green water,
they were eaten by minnows, bit by bit, moving between them

like sport. His innocence; his eyes. I reassembled him with the easy
conviction of a god, soothing physical connection, smoothing

breaks in the skin like gentle water over earth. I fashioned new eyes
from sycamore and polished bone and gently pressed them underneath

his lids. And I buried that body at Philoe, so his soul
was soon able to take another form. All that he really lost,

he would have lost anyway, at some time or another—sooner
or later. But I find it is hard to love a reassembled thing: hard to see it

as it is, and not as the pieces my hands have known
intimately; hard to see Osiris smiling, and not a confusion

of organs and limbs too fragile for excited talk, too delicate
for the daily strains of kindness or anger, my confidence or love.

Edgar at Supper, Fifty Years On
We that are young
Shall never see so much, nor live so long.
                                        —*King Lear*

I miss the misery. I knew I would, even as I leaped
away from my brother to the tribal drumming
of my heart: Britain was more ancient then, the stones
more palpably gray, our gods more resonant, more
actively above us. I ripped off my clothes, stuck
plants in my skin and for the first time was no heir
of anything
                except the evening; the marjoram
and hollyhock; the mud I rubbed over my cheeks
like rouge; just enough terror to crest my hesitation.

Well I have grandchildren now. Servants bring us
thoroughly cooked meat, and the table leg, the one
closest to my daughter, rests just on the spot
where my father's eyes were put out. A rug covers
that floor, and this table, that rug, and a fine sheath
of lace overlays the table. We cut our meat
in silence.
              The littlest ones look into their plates
and giggle about things I cannot even begin
to understand. They will still be children

when they see me buried by old men, last see me
laid out in the parlor, surrounded by black cloaks
and dresses, and everyone taking for granted
the luxury to mourn. One night by the fire, one
night soon, I may tell them something: how I stood
on a cliff and became a demon whose eyes
were moons, how I
                    thrust a sword through the bodies
of two men, one of whom was my brother, and though
the times seem so much more tranquil now, though I
seem so much more tranquil, how I hunched muddy

and naked, danced under the dark sky, and babbled
the truth from an uncensored heart. It is the time's
plague, children, when quiet silences us. But imagine
another time, when names were as loose, as fungible
as clothing, when sanity and identity fell
like tempestuous rain
                        and exposure to cold told us
how complicated it is to feel. My man comes
and refills my cup with wine: I nod, lift

the cup, mutter something, but my children, my
children's children, so used to me, do not even bother
to look up. "Another kingdom," I tell them, "brief,
incandescent, but so much more like living."

From the Shore

I look at the black lid of the Hellespont, wondering
if it has closed on you, or if you are close. When I see

you coming in the tower's light, I will run down
the steps, though when I become visible to you,

I shall begin to walk very slowly, so the moonlight
catches the wind in my hair and makes me as beautiful

as Andromeda, waiting out on the rock for the dragon.
I know what it means, you coming here—what risks

you take—and sometimes I decide for myself
that our love is worth those risks to you, and sometimes

I decide that our love is safe, protected by Aphrodite
and Eros, by the Fates, because it is true, and that Ocean

himself moves underneath you, mirrors your movement
to keep you from harm. Should I come as Andromeda,

or the one who wept so much she was turned into a wet
stone? The decision remains yours. I'll give you

whatever it is you come for, which isn't fear
that you'll die. You're too young to die. The sand

is warm tonight, and soft, and will be our bed until dawn.
I have a piece of coral for you, which I found walking

today, two cold apples and clear water. Also, I have me.
You must not think I don't know the distance from Sestos

to Abydos and how it changes in a thunderstorm;
that is why I love your arms most, and shoulders, why

I pray for them separately. Though I don't cross
with you, my risk is wedded to yours, and I don't sleep

for hours after you go, until I'm sure you have reached
shore. It is warm tonight, and the Hellespont is clear.

When I see your hair in the light, that's what we'll
talk about. We'll sit on a black jetty and look at the moon.

From the Water

I am fighting this Hellespont—a great definition of black
space below me, which I have traveled during storms

and on those few nights of the year it is cold. It continues
like a familiar argument to which there can be no logical

resolution, except those which contain their own undoing,
as the journey to Sestos necessitates the journey back,

and that, the journey out again. It is warm tonight, past
time for moonlight; I can still see stars when I turn

my head for breath, against the black sky, which
somewhere becomes the ocean. Miles from either shore,

sometimes I forget if I am heading to see you, or away,
though this traveling is always about you, and the salt

water seems to smell like you, and the wave swells feel
like you turning beneath me. Such swimming will take

my life eventually, in a storm I can't control, or by
the throwing up of hands, when I realize it's impossible

to mediate this distance between us and impossible to live
half the time with you and half away, and think always

of the black water and my arms which will eventually
tire. I thought tonight, before diving off the cliffs

of Abydos, about the lighthouse and you, and life
between two cities as different as sickness and health,

and decided to stay. But I found myself anyway
immersed in the water. I cannot remember if I have

seen you this evening, but I am sure you look—
or have looked—beautiful, that you felt as cool

and forceful as the strait, that the sounds you make
will be as constant. I have no doubt I love—or have

loved you—and also no doubt about the sand I will
catch my breath on, or the deep, black Hellespont.

Barely April

This is spring in my garden: five rows, a few pots,
and around the edges, flowers I can't name,

what I found at Kroger—small yellow suns,
or five red petals on a small bush-like stalk,

and others, long slender purple leaves
which shoot off flowers the exact same shade,

beautiful only through a lack of distinction.
This ground is full of glass shards. They appeared

when I ripped up the sod, and they appear
deeper and deeper, like layers of another

civilization. Before I came to this lawn, before
it grew, bottles shattered, maybe windows.

I think someone junked cars back here
and that explains the rusted bolts and screws.

The soil is good, though. It's barely April
and I've already harvested radishes and lettuce;

flowers are flourishing, and new seeds are in—
"sugar baby" and "homestead," maybe a matter

of months. But I won't be here then.
I'm leaving this house, leaving the lawn

I overturned, the pleasure I took
picking out glass, though it always seemed—

not hopeless, so much is growing here—
but endless. That was comforting, too.

I'll have to strike before fruition, the carrots,
onions—even though a few have already

started to bulb, and the bulbs
are breaking through. The landlords

leased a house without a garden, and that's
what they want back.
                           He and I are separating,

though he helped me build this.
So much stronger than I am, as much grass

as I overturned in an hour, he tripled
in half the time, formed rows—

even weeded though he barely fit
between them. He will live and I will, but not

together, and this is simple and easy,
as things must be when they're inevitable,

factual and specific like the secret details
of his infidelity: how many times, which positions,

what bookstores, what risk. I understand
no one uses condoms through a hole

in the wall, and of course not in our
bedroom either. I want to say our love

is like gardening—and the sense of upkeep
may be the same—but soil can't kill you.

Even filled with glass, it's the substance of life;
even taking lead from eight lanes of traffic,

this is a medium of becoming. Imagine,
tender lettuce roots wrap around bottle shards

and don't get cut. Perhaps it's the faith and patience
of slow growth which protects them. Soil

can transmute garbage, or contextualize it
into something harmless. Though it would come

slowly, though I wouldn't see it in a mirror,
this love may have cultured something else—

curling around my entrails like vines, locking
rib to rib, green leaves tickling under my heart.

This is the other garden I haven't seen (please
don't call it willful ignorance) and it seems

the perfect inverse of the first. Here the crop takes
the shape of a man, then takes that shape down.

There you start with soil; here you end with it.
Is it wrong for me not to want to leave?

Naive? These vines wreath between us, too,
and I find it difficult to change my picture of a man,

to say: not, "this is him, and this is what he has done,"
but, "this is him, and this is also him."

So the question will come—a matter of weeks,
when I buy sod, lift out the posts and prepare

to turn the soil, when I leave this house—
did I add anything to the bolts and glass?

Maybe something will come up for the next tenant—
seeds from the compost, onions in a curious row

that he or she won't eat. This is no
compensation.
                      Perhaps it's indulgence,

or simply weakness, to wander this paradise,
to touch the petals as if they will flower

and fruit. But this is spring in my garden;
it's cool and beautiful here, and my impulse is

to pretend—even if I know I can't sustain it—
to step through the lushness of so much

possibility and pretend I'll never have to leave.

Last Conversation in Monticello, NY

1.
Snow blowing in through the motel doorway, melting
on the red carpet. I lean down and pick up

the bag of milk, bread, chocolate, from where
you told me to leave it last night. Hard to believe

sometimes that hours move with equal friction,
that I have just met you and will soon make you

a stranger, or rather, we will make each other that way.
I unwrap the plastic cups and pour us out

glasses of half-frozen milk, break off some chocolate.
Is it permissible to kiss in daylight? The marks

on your neck are brighter now, but already
belong to fiction, to the stories we will tell

those people we've decided we know.
What is it you and I are moving towards? *Words.*

You are as beautiful as any man I've ever kissed.
Don't tell me that's all, only words. *Lonely words.*

2.
It's snowing heavily now, and though your drive
north will take hours, you decide there is time

for breakfast at the diner we met up at last night:
a cup of coffee, toasted bagel, and nothing

to say. Could you admit that sometimes intimacy
can spring like conversation, like light

from your fingertips? Shall I admit
I was awake for however long it was last night

that you ran your hand down my shoulder,
again and again, as if to retain the print

of my arm, the very sense of it on your palm?
Tell me, what will I do when I find myself

alone again? *Gain.* I could sit across from you
for days, staring through the curtain as the snow

mounts higher and higher against the glass.
What about my search for a lover? *All over.*

3.
You drop me off at the bus stop, snow obscuring
your windshield so that we feel comfortable

enough to kiss goodbye, as if you were
dropping me off for work. We are as separate

as mountains, and it is clear as I stand here
looking around in the snow—how it plates

everything in unsustainable shine, plays
sunlight to make even automobiles beautiful—

that our hours of conversation in the dark,
the truth, our hands, our bodies, all of it

will melt casually into our world of men,
like a conversation with yourself, or sex

with yourself. What would a mountain shout
to the surrounding air, and what would the air

echo in return? I could have loved you. *You?*
What can I be when I feel so broken? *Sober; oaken.*

Antonio Remembers Sebastian

How have you made division of yourself?
An apple cleft in two is not more twin
Than these two creatures. Which is Sebastian?
                              —*Twelfth Night*

1.
What could I have said? Once it became clear
for whom there was and was not a happy ending,
I took up silence the way I once took up the sea:
as both a medium and a solvent,
                              a pacifier
and my salvation. I have long understood
the narcosis of movement, the ability
to shake off the stiffness of my joints, to feel
as if my joints generated their own oil, and I
slowly come alive, a tin man.

Somehow this makes sense: coming awake
to my body let me fall asleep to memory.

2.
You have made division of yourself, Sebastian,
though you will not know it: mine is the dying
man I dredged up in the nets, his long red hair,
blue eyes swollen shut,
                              fingers crimped, mouthing
his sister's name. I breathed into his lips, then
the name he mouthed was mine. There is an intimacy
possible between men on the sea that makes no sense
on dry land, finds no words for what it is in the language
of heaviness and dirt.

You made no objection when I fed you. My purse
was yours, and we both belonged to the sea.

3.
I spy through the glass the shoreline of Illyria
and those neighboring lands where you are Duke.
This is the other you. But even then, I knew which
was Sebastian:
                the man with whom I rediscovered
the taste of salt water, found more than comfort
in its rocking rhythms. I have my own dukedom, now—
it is a principle of freedom defined by this vessel's
sweep up and down the coast that hems you in,
where I am a stranger

and also your jail keeper. My dukedom runs
circles around yours and remembers

the feel of your head on my chest. The body
of my dukedom washes up by the feet of yours

and just as insistently pulls back. It burns
wounds clean and swallows human death.

4.
Not all players were meant to have a happy ending,
even in comedy. I know that. Once self-awareness
shook off this scripted silence—even Feste
was allowed a song, even
                            Malvolio a final curse—
I understood my cue for movement, the pathway
clear, off the thrust stage of our life together,
a small back exit to the sea: exit Antonio—
to where there is absence, where there was
no absence; to where

Illyria dominates all coastlines, a land mass
as imposing as hope. There remains

some little peace in movement
and in understanding that this is my part.

Renaissance Fair

We played in the pillory. You remember.
                                            You ate a turkey leg,
ripping the meat off like a barbarian, barbecue sauce on your
unshaven face, your shirt. We kissed in the cathedral. Our
ancient Authors doe conclude, that it deſerueth death,
though they differ
                        in the manner of puniſhment. I spread
my long hair on your lap, under the wood-beam skeleton
grown over with blue-flowering ivy. Sun
                                        filtered through, lit
the dust around your eyes. You touched
                                            my hair; you felt
me up. It was like no one was there, though men and women
around us drank beer and kissed in their own stone pews.
So as there muſt be
                        penetratio, that is, either with mankind, or
beaſt, but the leaſt penetration maketh it carnall knowledge.
We strolled out of the village, passed the jousting grounds,
the green and red knights. I tried on a garland of flowers and
Emiſio ſeminis maketh it not Buggery, but is an evidence
the saleswoman laughed.
                            in caſe of buggery of penetration.
We played in the pillory. You even took a picture
of me grinning, wristwatch poking through the wooden stocks,
glasses crooked on my face, the crowd milling behind me.
Britton ſaith, that Sodomites ſhall be
                                    You won money on
the white rat.
        burnt and ſo were the Sodomites by Almighty God.
Then it was twilight, the ground littered with Miller Lite
cans, a band of squires shepherding us
                                          See the indictment
of Stafford committing buggery with a boy,
                                            toward the door.
for which he was hanged. We walked across the parking lot

and found ourselves followed by a dozen men and women.
One was yelling. Buggery is a deteſtable
                                            "Are you
faggots? Which one of you fucks the other your dicks got to be
pretty small how else you get it in a hole that small?"
I reached up grabbed you by the head and brought your face
to mine, a kiss that banged our teeth together. One of them
spat on us. There were more than a dozen.
                                        They differ
We starting walking again.
                        in the manner of puniſhment.
The crowd moved passed us. deteſtable
                                        They followed
and surrounded us. and abominable sin. One of them
grabbed my hips and pushed me down. Amongst
                                            They
spat on me. Christians. I picked myself up. *Inter Chriſtianos*
And began to run.
            non nominandum. So did you.
                                        Not
They laughed at us
                not to be named. and they let us run.

Zharkov, Discovered in 1997, Translated Sometime After the Year 2000

Besides analyzing dirt, pollen, and even its stomach contents, a primary task is to extract DNA for cloning. . . .
—AP, 10/21/99

1.
It has been twenty-three ages encased in ice. I do not remember;
my body remembers and informs me: tells in an ache which echoes
into these new limbs from a distant pattern, a tiny photon
of information brightening inside each cell.
                                          This second birth
feels like a defrosting, cold limbs remembering pliability,
a cold heart remembering (from twenty-three ages before
I was remade) warmth.

I was moved in a block of ice, found with just my tusks
breaking the surface of a world in which all things live and die,
ivory polished by the wind of a thousand human generations.
My least sensate part bore
                                  each day's weather, what would have
devoured me, while not removing me from life as it manifests itself
in other things, would have removed the possibility
from me.

But someone found my tusks and projected something
underneath the ice; a scientist bent to feel my hair.

2.
I was carried to the only environment that could sustain me,
a cave in Khatanga, the coldest part of our planet, but still not
cold enough. There a dozen men in lab coats worked
over me, thawing each piece, searching
                                          through what the cold
had left preserved if dehydrated: powdered mulch
in my stomach, dry waste in my bowels, impulses of death
a fine silt

dusting my brain, like a fall of very dry snow. Those thoughts
are gone. Yet they are here in a body which remembers
inside each cell; they animate desire, a stiff muscle
that bends, cracks, and overcomes the stiffness.
                                        My rough skin,
its hair coarse as thick hemp, recovers feeling as from the cracking
in spring, but still somehow retains its weight as armor.
Those thoughts

of death live in the motions of this body, the musculature
structuring my flesh, the ability to run and trumpet
to a frozen universe, which may or may not respond in kind.

3.
I was numb to the pain of dissection, the search for what I
could not see though it was clearly mine: an intact string
of information, a model of what I was meant to be, that might
enable a restructuring of the whole.
                        I cannot say
what it felt like to have hands reach inside my numb body,
where there is pain and yet numbness, cannot explain the scraping
of my powdered blood.

But something remained in the spheres of dry white ice
which were my eyes, the crumbling leather of my liver,
lungs and heart. And they pulled it out of me, found
what I was
            had stayed cold until I was ready to live, reborn
in a world of spring. I cannot hold this technology, cannot like it,
but it has animated

the heart of a desiccated thing. Spring on top of the world
is colder and there are no flowers. I relearn what to eat
in a context of hyperconsciousness: where all men wear
lab coats. My world is bound
                                by the science that remade me,
but elegant with formations of ice. You would not know it,
you'd feel it

like cold: but this thick skin feels freedom, this dry heart
blood, and though each cell is full and cannot help but
enact its inheritance, my thoughts, my thoughts feel new.

Amerigo Vespucci, 1506, Contemplates Another Sheet of Vellum

I was there. I saw the mouth of the Amazon, its tongue
of water sticking out into the Atlantic, trying to turn
its blue babble into speech. I saw Guanabara Bay.
When no living thing had ever recorded seeing it, I saw it—
and imagined the inlet lit by spires, imagined the voice
of Pope and Emperor as towers pushed to the edge
of the water, bright at night . . . boats sailing the bay. In short,
I saw a city there, the crossing of boats in the crossing of birds,
towers in the trees.
     I saw it from deck; I saw it from the sand
which winnowed between my fingers, which spread out
in the air like chaff; I almost see it in my head now, and struggle
to lean my head back from my desk, to feel on my face
the heat of a meridian sun.

But this is painful. Here are two empty pages. On one
I must draw a map. Each line will condense entire weeks:
here, I plot a vector of coast, and you look at it, admire
its clean simplicity. That simplicity is a fabrication. What you
don't see from the elevation gradients is how the cliff bled
a shadow on the pale water, dyeing it black, how I
misconstrued the distance and just barely turned the vessel
about in time. You have part of what you want here—
the destination—but you have it clean. And this is not natural:
to record experience
     filtered through experience,
to make sure all the lines form only a single continent.
On this other page I must write a narrative. Truth may be
unavoidable, may exist on a continental scale. But you want
only that truth

which you can discover yourself. Not just the map, but
the evolution of the map, so that you can make the journey,
can rig up the boat of your imagination—so all Europe
can hitch their parlors to the keel of my ship and be

dragged over the ocean. And this too is artifice.
If the destination involves shaping a flip book of glances
into a coherent picture, then this requires breaking coherence
back into steps. So the chair under me is leather; the desk
in front of me is wood. But the world before me must be
the world I have left—
                      I must be there again, and here,
and still trying to reenter and reconstruct the voyage, to parse
a moonlit journey by lamplight, smell the wet air of morning
on Rio de la Plata and remember how the glinting sun
brought to mind a river of silver. . . .

Artifice is our general burden. This continent of experience,
the geographical features of discovery and desire, they exist
only so far as they are shared. So I was there. Every line,
every nautical mile: the book will map myself, too—
as I stood on deck, as I sit at this desk, as I walk
the streets of Seville thinking about where best to place
the color plates. But I can claim nothing in the experience,
nothing in the book, that you are not able to follow yourself.
In other words, so far as I can claim it is real, I promise:
the continent is also yours.
                      So I dip into the ink and start
another page. Without a visitation or a miracle,
that world will remain two thousand miles away.
You I imagine; the continent I remember. The rest
is in the hands of God.

Conclusion of a Poem Begun By Marlowe
without apologies to Chapman

The strait reeled up, and Leander could feel himself
lifted twenty, thirty feet on one surge, from off the dark water
into the black sky and the storm. He was a tiny thing
struggling in the mouth of enormity, beating his hands
with even time into the salt water, trying to maintain
a sense of separation between the wildness of the storm—
the crash in his ear, his body tossed up and fighting,
and then the danger, down into another wave—
and what he pictured as another ocean within: this one
also black on black, also with Hero on one side of it
wringing her reedy arms, but here, calm upon calm,
emptiness above and below a flat horizon, a seam
on which he was moving forward.
                                   Toward what?
Inside there was only movement. Sestos existed
on the outside: with the cymbal crashes and splits
of light that showed him how high he was, how far
he was about to be thrown by the wave, showed him
the next wave like a black tooth as it reared and fell
into him. Inside the swimming was steady and even,
and there was room to hold a thousand oceans. Inside
he could stand above the storm, see it at as a tantrum
in a tea cup, splash out its little fury with his finger.
He was aware also of a small irony: that only the thinness
of his skin kept these two worlds from somehow
contaminating each other, a mixing of scale which might
destroy both. But maybe containment wouldn't be possible
much longer.
              Now, in his inner ocean: there was Hero,
flushed with shame from this morning, tender with blood
if not with virtue, unable to bring herself to touch him
with her fingers. All anticlimax somehow.
But she was there, receding by a single lamp, removed
by two continents. Leander was plunged beneath the salt,

and half the Hellespont seemed to wash above his head,
but his arms mechanically beat their way back up,
and his head broke the surface just at that moment
bright with lightning. He seemed to crest a hundred feet
above Greece, high enough to grab a foot of the golden
sheep had it been flying by at that moment, and he
gulped air and glimpsed himself about to slam down
under a wave.
          Now, in his inner ocean: someone else
was there, too. A shape he hadn't quite realized before,
at least not in this way. It was a man, suddenly come
into the light on the opposite shore. Or maybe not shore,
but in a place different than Hero. The man's skin was pale
blue with an oil sheen, and his eyes were heavily lidded.
After a moment, the man silently lifted a webbed hand
to Leander, to pull him closer. Leander felt himself moving.
As he approached, the figure became larger and larger
until Leander was standing before a man whose embrace
could crush his body. This image so absorbed him
that he wasn't aware that he'd stopped swimming, or that,
thrown deep inside a wave, he was losing valuable seconds
necessary to pull himself out.
          No, this man was trying to
tell him something. Leander came closer, toward the blue
hand with its darker blue fingernails, toward the hand
strangely etched with winesap veins. The figure bent
over him then, and leaned his face down close to Leander's.
The taste was familiar: wind and salt water.
          But gentle now,
brushing his nose and pulsing around his lips—
easy, nothing worth fighting, no stinging or gagging.
"Now will you let me tell you a story?" the man said,
"about a shepherd and a boy fairer than Ganymede?"
The man's lips were maroon, almost the color of berry syrup,
and they moved mere inches from his own. For a moment
Leander heard a voice back over his shoulder, a single cry
from the opposite shore. It was Hero, standing up
by her candle, but her voice was a million miles away.

Yes, thought Leander, tell me your story. And though
he intended listening, he opened his mouth instead,
right near Neptune's, and felt the sea god come rushing in.

One Last Thought

And what if one finally can't be found? What if Leander
decides to make another choice?
                                        Is there a myth

of a man who walks out to the shore and stares at it
so long that he forgets himself and eventually is forgotten
even by gods? He's still there, five ages after
his civilization has become only traces in stone.

Or how about a man who thinks he sees a water nymph,
but instead of being drawn into the water after her,

he squints and stares as the Aegean sun
                                        bleaches
his bones beneath his skin. He squints and stares

as the years waste him away, until Aphrodite takes pity
on unfulfilled desire and turns him into a conch shell,
recessing inward in ever decreasing spirals, filled only
with the compensating thrum of the ocean.

And the wood nymph who loved him? The Goddess
turned her into a hermit crab—
                                      sometimes she finds him out

and fills his endless declivity like a muffle in a horn,
tuning him to love, bringing him along for a while.

The Richard Snyder Publication Series

This book is the ninth book in a series honoring the memory of Richard Snyder (1925-1986), poet, fiction writer, playwright and longtime professor of English at Ashland University. Snyder served for fifteen years as English Department chair, and was co-founder (in 1969) and co-editor of the Ashland Poetry Press, an adjunct of the university. He was also co-founder of the Creative Writing major at the school, one of the first on the undergraduate level in the country. In selecting the manuscript for this book, the editors kept in mind Snyder's tenacious dedication to craftsmanship and thematic integrity.

Snyder Award Winners:
1997: Wendy Battin for *Little Apocalypse*
1998: David Ray for *Demons in the Diner*
1999: Philip Brady for *Weal*
2000: Jan Lee Ande for *Instructions for Walking on Water*
2001: Corrinne Clegg Hales for *Separate Escapes*
2002: Carol Barrett for *Calling in the Bones*
2003: Vern Rutsala for *The Moment's Equation*
2004: Christine Gelineau for *Remorseless Loyalty*
2005: Benjamin S. Grossberg for *Underwater Lengths in a Single Breath*
2006: Lorna Knowles Blake for *Permanent Address*